W9-BHB-635

MONSTER MUSIC FESTIVALS™

COACHELLA

GREG ROBISON

rosen publishing's
rosen central®

New York

This one is for Mark, David, and Michael Sherman; the gang at B&N; Roger, Gina, Chris, Tricia, and Ken at Rosen; and, of course, Kelly Rae.

Published in 2009 by The Rosen Publishing Group, Inc.
29 East 21st Street, New York, NY 10010

Library of Congress Cataloging-in-Publication Data

Robison, Greg.
Coachella / Greg Robison.
    p. cm.—(Monster music festivals)
Includes bibliographical references (p. 46) and index.
ISBN-13: 978-1-4042-1755-3 (library binding)
ISBN-13: 978-1-4358-5120-7 (pbk)
ISBN-13: 978-1-4042-7865-3 (6 pack)
1. Coachella Valley Music and Arts Festival—Juvenile literature. 2. Rock music festivals—California—Indio—Juvenile literature. I. Title.
ML38.I53C639 2009
781.64079'79497—dc22

                                                                                2007051926

Manufactured in Malaysia

On the cover: Foreground, left: Willie Nelson at Coachella 2007; foreground, right: Kanye West at Coachella 2006. Background, top row, left to right: scene from 2007; fiery art installation, 2007; cheering fans, 2007; Amy Winehouse, 2007. Background, right, top to bottom: Madonna, 2006; Cansei de Ser Sexy, 2007; Anthony Kiedis of the Red Hot Chili Peppers, 2007.

CONTENTS

INTRODUCTION

Frank Black *(left)*, guitarist and lead vocalist for the Pixies, at Coachella in 2004. Flea, Chad Smith, and John Frusciante *(above, from left to right)* of the Red Hot Chili Peppers jam at Coachella in 2007.

You're lost in the Mojave Desert one day in late spring, and you come upon a beautiful valley. But this isn't just any valley. There are famous bands playing diverse types of music on different stages. There are artists from all over the world displaying their beautiful works. There are hundreds of booths set up where vendors are selling unique clothing, music, books, and many other interesting items. And thousands of people are on hand, enjoying themselves all day and night. Is it a mirage? Have you been in the sun too long? Nope, you have stumbled across the annual Coachella Valley Music and Arts Festival!

The Coachella Valley Music and Arts Festival (usually referred to as Coachella Fest, or just Coachella), is a two-day event that is held annually at the Empire Polo Field in beautiful Indio, California. Indio is located approximately fifty miles (eighty kilometers) from the famed Mojave Desert. If you had to describe the Coachella Fest in just one word, it would be "diverse." There is truly something for everyone to see, hear, and do at this festival. It is where music, art, and film lovers come together. Bands from all musical genres are represented at Coachella, including alternative rock, rap/hip-hop,

indie, and electronica. International superstars such as Rage Against the Machine, the Red Hot Chili Peppers, Beck, Jane's Addiction, Oasis, and Tool have performed at the festival. In addition, world-renowned artists and filmmakers show their creations at Coachella. You can take a break from the heat and catch a screening of a brand-new film, even before it hits movie theaters. Or, you can stroll around the festival grounds and view some of the beautiful scenery that surrounds Coachella.

The Coachella Festival celebrated its eighth year in 2007. It is considered by many to be the best music and art festival of its kind. Put on your sunscreen and read on to learn more about this incredible festival.

CHAPTER 1

OVERCOMING OBSTACLES:

THE HISTORY OF COACHELLA

How did one of the hottest and driest places in all America become the home of one of the world's most popular music festivals?

Rocking the Desert: The First Coachella Festival

In 1993, alternative rockers Pearl Jam and Tool were searching for a venue to play a concert that wouldn't cost their fans a lot of money. They could not have chosen a more unlikely place than the Empire Polo Field in Indio, California. It's really hot in Indio, and there was also the matter of its location: it's between a one- and five-hour drive from larger cities such as Los Angeles, Las Vegas, Phoenix, and San Diego.

To the delight of everyone involved, the concert was a huge success. On the evening of November 5, 1993, more than

At the height of their popularity, Pearl Jam (shown here, in 1993) played a concert at the Empire Polo Field in Indio, California—the future home of the Coachella Festival.

twenty-five thousand fans sat or stood on the grounds of the previously rock-festival-free Empire Polo Field. Everyone seemed to love the beautiful surroundings of Indio. It was the start of bigger and better things to come.

Fast-forward six years to 1999. This didn't appear to be the greatest of times to start a brand-new music festival. In July of that year, the disastrous Woodstock 1999 festival occurred.

Outrageous pricing on food and water, poor security, and unsanitary conditions led to riots and fires started by frustrated festival attendees. In a *USA Today* interview from July 29, 1999, MTV host Kurt Loder described the debacle: "The whole scene was scary," he said, "with waves of hatred bouncing around. It was clear we had to get out of there." MTV, which had been providing live coverage of the festival, removed its whole crew.

Promoters of the Coachella Festival wisely vowed not to make the same mistakes. Their goal was to create an environment that was fan-friendly. They wanted to provide a clean, safe environment, with ample security and restrooms that were cleaned and restocked regularly (a music festival first!). They didn't want to charge attendees an arm and a leg for food and beverages. Prices would be very reasonable, and all festival-goers would even get a free bottle of water to keep cool. And they wanted to provide something different for everyone who came out to the show: diverse genres of music, interesting art exhibits, and film exhibitions. This would be a festival that people would want to return to each year. And on October 9–10, 1999, a mere three months after the Woodstock '99 fiasco, the Coachella Festival was launched.

As with the original Pearl Jam/Tool concert six years earlier, some critics were concerned that Indio was too remote a location to host a music festival. They needn't have worried: the two-day event drew almost twenty-five thousand people! People came from all over to see such bands as Rage Against the Machine,

Beck, a groundbreaking musician and singer, performs at the very first Coachella Festival in 1999.

Tool, A Perfect Circle, Jurassic 5, the Chemical Brothers, and Pavement, along with solo performances from such artists as Beck, Perry Farrell, Moby, and Morrissey. Additionally, more than thirty other bands from all genres of music rocked the first festival.

Thanks to great planning, an incredible band lineup, and a clean, comfortable venue, Coachella was viewed as a success by the majority of people that attended it. The only concern was the blistering heat. Unfortunately, that first festival failed to generate a profit for the promoters who worked so hard to put it on. This means that they spent more money on running Coachella than they made on ticket and concession sales. Some changes were going to have to be made if the festival was going to continue, along with getting some help from a famous friend.

A Friend Indeed: Perry Farrell Helps Save Coachella 2001

The promoters of Coachella Fest elected not to put on the festival in 2000. There were concerns about how they could maintain high standards and an incredible music lineup while still generating a modest profit for all of their efforts. It was decided that "the show must go on" in 2001. Wisely, they moved Coachella to April, to avoid the intense heat of later months, and they shortened the festival to a one-day format.

Several months prior to the show, the promoters were concerned about the artist lineup. True, they had established acts such as Weezer, Radiohead, the Roots, Iggy Pop, and the Orb on the bill. But they felt they were missing that one blockbuster act, a band that folks absolutely could not miss. Enter Perry Farrell.

To most music fans, Perry Farrell is a name associated with innovative music, outrageous live shows, and Lollapalooza. He was the visionary front man of Jane's Addiction, a band that helped bring grunge and metallic punk rock to the mainstream. In 1991, Farrell founded Lollapalooza, one of the very first traveling alternative rock festivals, as a farewell tribute tour for Jane's Addiction. This wildly popular festival toured North America through 1997, and it is now an annual event held in Chicago, Illinois.

In 2001, the promoters of Coachella were running out of time, and they still needed a headliner band for the festival.

Masterful entertainer Perry Farrell leads his band, Jane's Addiction, at the 2001 Coachella Festival.

They turned to Farrell (who had made a solo appearance at the 1999 Coachella Festival), in hopes that he might have some suggestions. He didn't disappoint them. Not only did Farrell agree to perform at the festival, he reunited the legendary Jane's Addiction for the show. This surprise move was just what Coachella needed. In the end, the 2001 show was a big success, and Coachella was back in business.

Coachella Generates Worldwide Interest

In 2002, Coachella returned to its original two-day format. And it's a good thing, too, because the music lineup that year was amazing. People came in droves to see such bands as Foo Fighters, the Strokes, Queens of the Stone Age, the Vines,

Cake, the Mars Volta, and Oasis. The highlight of the festival was the reunion of UK punk darlings Siouxsie and the Banshees. The strong band lineup and smooth operation of the festival convinced the people of Indio that Coachella could be a good thing for their community, bringing in revenue and generating positive attention.

In 2003, huge crowds came for the reunion of Detroit legends the Stooges, led by Iggy Pop. The Red Hot Chili Peppers and the Beastie Boys also headlined the show. But it was the epic 2004 show that started turning heads around the world. That year was the festival's first complete sellout, with all fifty thousand tickets sold on both Saturday and Sunday. Festival attendees witnessed performances from such acts as the Cure, Radiohead, and Kraftwerk, and yet another reunited band, the Pixies. The Coachella Festival was creating quite a name for itself with its incredible artist lineups, art and movie exhibits, and beautiful surroundings. People everywhere wanted to check out the show for themselves.

The Reunion Factor: What Makes Coachella Unique?

The music industry is very challenging. Being in a successful band requires a lot of hard work and effort. Bands put in long days in the studio to record their music, and they spend a great deal of time away from home, family, and friends when they are on tour. As a result, many bands get burned out and decide

to break up. Sometimes the breakup is a permanent one, and sometimes it is just what is called a hiatus—when a band doesn't record, tour, or play together for a period. So, it's always a highly anticipated event when a popular band decides to reunite for a concert performance or tour, or to record some new music.

Since 2001, when Jane's Addiction reunited, it has become something of a Coachella tradition to reunite at least one band to perform at each year's festival. Several groups have reunited

For many fans, seeing the Pixies perform together again was the highlight of the 2004 Coachella Festival.

at Coachella or have played the festival as one of their first major shows following a reunion. Below is a list of performers who have gotten back together or made a big return at the Coachella Festival:

2001 Jane's Addiction
2002 Siouxsie and the Banshees
2003 Iggy and the Stooges
2004 The Pixies
2005 Bauhaus; Gang of Four
2006 Daft Punk (their first U.S. performance since 1997); Tool (their first live show in three years)
2007 Rage Against the Machine; Crowded House; the Happy Mondays

CHAPTER 2

Too Hot to Handle:

The Coachella Festival Setting

If you are planning on attending the Coachella Festival, be sure to pack the sunscreen. The festival is held annually at the Empire Polo Field in Indio, California, where temperatures regularly rise above one hundred degrees Fahrenheit (thirty-eight degrees Celsius) during the day. The good news is that after the sunset, the temperature drops drastically.

Hello, Indio!

Indio is located in the Coachella Valley of Southern California. The Mojave Desert begins a mere fifty miles (eighty kilometers) north of Indio. The town was founded in 1894 when the railroad chose the remote area as a train stop, due to the fact that it was the halfway point between Los Angeles, California, and Yuma, Arizona. The community was named for the Native American

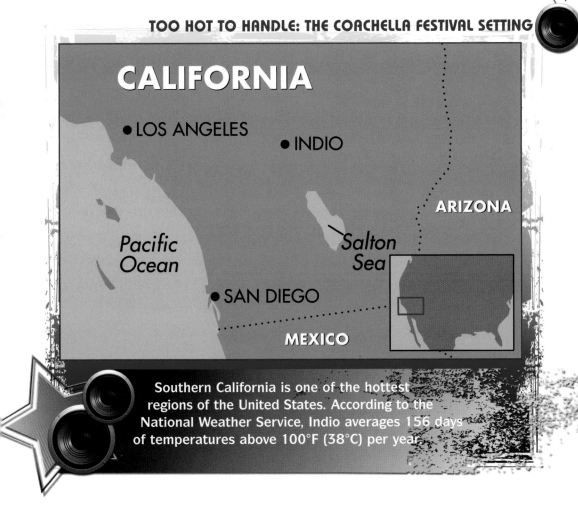

CALIFORNIA

• LOS ANGELES

• INDIO

*Pacific
Ocean*

*Salton
Sea*

ARIZONA

• SAN DIEGO

MEXICO

Southern California is one of the hottest regions of the United States. According to the National Weather Service, Indio averages 156 days of temperatures above 100°F (38°C) per year.

Indians who lived in the area during railroad construction. (*Indio* is Spanish for "Indian.") Today, more than fifty thousand people call Indio home.

At first glance, the small, remote agricultural center of Indio is one of the last places that you would think of to host one of the world's largest annual music festivals. When people say Indio is a hot place to host a festival, they mean it literally!

 COACHELLA

When you're just forty-five minutes away from one of the largest deserts in America, you can expect things to be a little toasty.

Music fans from all around the county first became aware of this desert community in 1993. That year, two of the biggest bands in the world decided to play a show at the Empire Polo Field in Indio. At the height of their popularity, Pearl Jam and Tool attracted more than twenty-five thousand fans to the desert location. And since 1999, the Coachella Festival has called Indio home, making it an annual destination for music fans from around the globe. People have fallen in love with Indio's desert surroundings. In fact, *Rolling Stone* magazine named Indio as one of the most beautiful music festival sites in the world.

Eye Candy: What You Will See at the Coachella Festival

When you first enter the front gates of the Coachella Festival, you might think you are at an art gallery or special museum. While music is the main feature of Coachella, there are many people who come to the festival each year to experience the beautiful and unique art exhibits. You can check out some awesome sculpture art, with works featured at exhibits throughout the festival grounds. In addition, each year, Coachella invites famous installation and performance artists from all over the world to set up their exhibits around the festival grounds. In an installation art exhibit, you might find

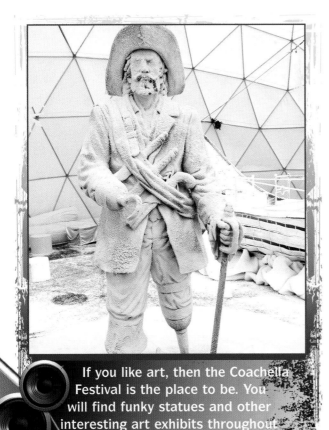

If you like art, then the Coachella Festival is the place to be. You will find funky statues and other interesting art exhibits throughout the festival grounds.

sculpture materials, along with other everyday objects and natural materials. Most of these installations are considered "new media" projects, meaning that they also involve video, sound, live performers, and computers. Many installations are also interactive, providing an added layer of entertainment to people strolling the festival grounds. Highly regarded installation artists you may see at Coachella include:

- Cyclecide
- Robochrist Industries
- Kinetic Steam Works
- The Mutaytor
- The Do Lab

If you're in the mood for a movie, you can catch a film while you're at the festival. Movie producers and directors from across the globe debut their latest works at Coachella each year. Take a movie break between your favorite bands and you may see a future Academy Award winner before its nationwide release.

Be sure to bring your appetite to Coachella. You can find an international variety of good eats at booths located throughout the festival grounds. Sample some European cuisine from the restaurant in the European village. Go south of the border with some excellent Mexican food, or sample some delicious pan-Asian dishes. If it's traditional American food that you crave, there are several restaurants and snack bars on site to please your taste buds as well. *Bon appétit!*

The incredible art exhibits, premier movie screenings, and international foods are all an important part of Coachella. But let's not forget the main focus of the festival, which is the music.

Ear Candy: The Music of the Coachella Festival

Since 1999, the Coachella Festival has featured strong music lineups from the opening act to the festival headliner. This is what has helped the festival grow from twenty-five thousand attendees in 1999, to more than one hundred thousand fans at the 2007 show. Famous musicians, as well as up-and-coming artists from around the world, appear at the festival each year. Various genres, or types, of music are represented at Coachella.

Alternative Rock

Also known as alternative music, or simply alternative, alternative rock started in the 1980s and became widely popular in the 1990s. Alternative music is influenced by punk rock, hard rock, folk music, reggae, and even jazz. Heavy guitars, gothic soundscapes, and the ringing guitar sounds of British pop are just some of the sounds that you will hear in alternative rock. Some examples of alternative rock bands that have played Coachella are Tool, Rage Against the Machine, Jane's Addiction, the Red Hot Chili Peppers, Coldplay, and the Cure.

Electronica

Electronica is an umbrella term describing music that emphasizes the use of electronic musical instruments and computer technology. Subgenres of electronica include techno, drum and bass, acid house, and trance music. Electronica artists that have performed at Coachella include Daft Punk, the Prodigy, the Chemical Brothers, and the Orb.

Hip-Hop

Hip-hop can be described as both a musical genre and a cultural movement. After springing from New York in the 1970s and 1980s, hip-hop music and culture spread around the world. The music contains elements of rap, music sampling, emceeing, and deejaying. Hip-hop artists who have rocked the

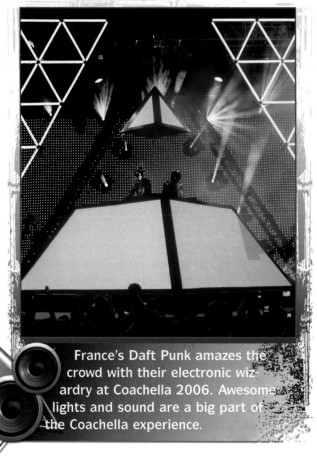

France's Daft Punk amazes the crowd with their electronic wizardry at Coachella 2006. Awesome lights and sound are a big part of the Coachella experience.

house at Coachella include the Black Eyed Peas, Mos Def, the Pharcyde, and G. Love & Special Sauce.

Sets and Stages

In 2007, more than one hundred bands performed at Coachella during a three-day period. That's a lot of tunes! The first bands generally crank it up between 1:00 and 2:00 PM, and the music continues until midnight. Artists perform sets ranging from forty-five minutes to almost two hours in length. Coachella has a total of five stages that artists perform on: the Coachella Stage, the Outdoor Theatre Stage, the Mojave Stage, the Gobi Stage, and the Sahara Stage.

The first stage you see when you enter Coachella is the Coachella Stage. The Outdoor Theatre Stage is located to the right of the Coachella Stage. To keep with the desert theme of Coachella, the Gobi, Mojave, and Sahara are referred to as "tent stages" because they all have giant tents surrounding them. These three stages are located in a row to the far right of the Outdoor Theatre. All stages have plenty of space between them so that you won't hear five bands playing all at once.

There are generally seven to nine bands performing on each stage every day of the festival. The Coachella Stage is what's known as the main stage of the festival, where the headliners and the bigger bands usually play. For example, in 2007, you would have seen Rage Against the Machine, Björk, the Red Hot Chili Peppers, and Willie Nelson on the Coachella Stage. However, the other four stages always feature great artists and big names as well. Each stage is equipped with state-of-the-art production and lighting, so you are treated to a great listening experience wherever you go.

CHAPTER 3

MAKING IT HAPPEN:

THE PEOPLE OF THE COACHELLA FESTIVAL

Many music fans and artists say Coachella is the one music festival that they'd prefer to attend or perform at each year. This enthusiasm is one of the main reasons why people keep coming back every year and bands hope to be invited to play.

Another Sellout: Who Attends the Coachella Festival?

Since 2004, the Coachella Festival has been a complete sellout. More than fifty thousand tickets were sold for each day of the two-day festival in both 2004 and 2005. In 2006, more than 120,000 people were in attendance over the festival weekend, thanks largely to pop diva Madonna's first appearance at Coachella. However, all previous attendance records were shattered in 2007, when the festival expanded to three days.

Fun goes on round the clock at the Coachella Festival. Here, fans at the 2006 festival mill about, waiting for the next great performance.

An average of sixty thousand fans flocked to the desert each day to witness performances by more than 120 bands, including the mighty, reunited Rage Against the Machine.

It's not just people from the United States who attend Coachella. Festival-goers come from Mexico and Canada, Europe, Australia, Asia, and South America to enjoy the sights and sounds. Coachella is an all-ages show, so everyone can attend the festival. However, you have to be at least eighteen years old in order to stay overnight at the festival campgrounds.

Coachella attendees enjoy a wide variety of music. You will see fans of pop, indie rock, rap/hip-hop, electronica, alternative rock, heavy metal, and country music at the different stages all throughout the festival.

Will Work for Tickets: Working at the Coachella Festival

With so many people attending Coachella each year, it takes a lot of hard work from many people to make sure everything runs smoothly. Of course, the army of festival workers includes the people needed for any music concert—bands, managers, roadies, and security guards. But some jobs at Coachella are unique to the festival. Here are a few of them:

Water Bottle Recycling Attendant

It gets hot at Coachella—really hot. It's important that you drink plenty of water while having fun in the blistering sun. That's why one person has one of the most popular jobs at the festival. The recycling attendant collects used water bottles from thirsty fans. For every ten empty bottles a person brings to the booth, the attendant exchanges them for a brand-new bottle of ice-cold water. Helping keep the festival grounds clean, being environmentally friendly, and giving out free water—what a great gig!

Sculptor

There are some truly amazing works of art on display at the Coachella Festival. You will be certain to see something that catches your eye as you walk through the festival grounds. Sculptors are the artists responsible for creating these amazing pieces. Coachella's sculptors work with clay, wood, cloth, metal, and plastics, and they shape or mold them into interesting three-dimensional objects.

Carpool Spotter

This is a truly unique and fun job at Coachella. The festival encourages all attendees to be kind to the environment. Carpooling helps reduce the amount of pollution emitted into the air by cars and trucks. Carpool spotters are located in the parking lots that surround Coachella. They look for people in cars with special "Carpoolchella" signs on their vehicles, indicating that they have carpooled to the show with at least four people in the car. The spotters select certain carpoolers at random and award them Coachella passes—for life! Giving people lifetime passes to one of the greatest festivals in the world, just for being environmentally smart—it doesn't get more rewarding than that.

Campsite "Counselor"

Many who attend Coachella also camp out during the festival. The camping area is directly next to the festival entrance and is located on beautiful, lush green grass. The campsite also features sparkling clean restrooms, free showers, a general store, and even a nightclub that hosts entertainment for campers, including movies and karaoke. Camp counselors help folks check in when they arrive at the campsite. They can help you if you can't find your campsite or if you need directions to the festival.

You won't really be "roughing it" at the Coachella Festival campgrounds. The camping area boasts spotless facilities, free showers, an on-site store, and even a nightclub!

Counselors also help keep the campsites clean and enforce rules and regulations.

Tow Truck Driver

With well more than one hundred thousand folks attending Coachella now, there's a good chance that some attendees are going to experience car trouble or lock their keys in their car. Tow truck drivers are located throughout the festival parking lots to help people get back on the road again. They help people change tires, jump-start car batteries, or transport cars with more serious problems to local auto repair shops.

Festival Photographer

Festival photographers work for newspapers, for music magazines and publications, and for bands. They take pictures of the musicians performing, the festival surroundings, and the people who attend the show. They use the most advanced cameras and equipment to make sure they take the best pictures possible. Additionally, they are issued special "Photo Access" passes that allow them to go virtually anywhere at the festival.

Information Booth Attendant

With so much to see and do at Coachella, many people will have questions regarding the festival. Information booth attendants are the "one-stop shop" for all inquiries, so they have to know almost everything about the festival. They can help folks with directions, band start times, food recommendations, and many other practical considerations.

First-Aid Tent Personnel

You might be having so much fun at Coachella rocking with your favorite bands that you get a little overheated. Or, maybe the heat has made you feel dehydrated. Don't delay! Go and see the good folks in the first-aid tent who are ready and willing to help you out. Always open during the show, they can treat your minor injuries or just give you a place to lie down and cool off. They will have you up and rocking again in no time. Also, special shade tents are located throughout the festival grounds to help you keep cool.

You may be interested in working one of these unique and rewarding jobs at the Coachella Festival. Or, maybe you would

This is the home page of the official Coachella Web site (www.coachella.com). Go here for the latest news on the festival.

like to volunteer to help make the show a huge success. Check out the official Web site at www.coachella.com; the festival organizers will always post job openings when something becomes available.

CHAPTER 4
A DAY (AND NIGHT) TO REMEMBER:
THE COACHELLA FESTIVAL EXPERIENCE

I f you are lucky enough to get hooked up with tickets for the Coachella Festival, get ready to have a blast. You are in for a truly amazing festival experience. With more than one hundred bands playing over the weekend, cool artwork to check out, and plenty of options for movies and other activities, you're going to stay busy. So, be sure that you rest up the night before the show.

Getting Ready to Rock: Preparing for Coachella

Before you head out to Coachella, here are a few tips to help you have a safe and enjoyable time. The night before the show, go to www.coachella.com and select the "interact" icon. Scroll down to the "coachooser" selection, and it will allow you to create a customized schedule for the festival so you won't

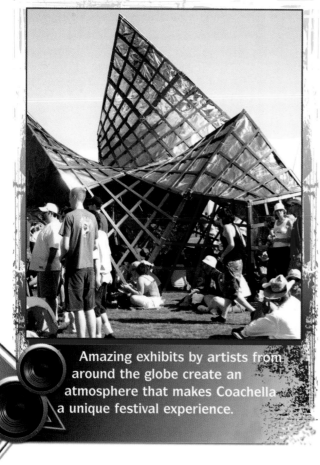

Amazing exhibits by artists from around the globe create an atmosphere that makes Coachella a unique festival experience.

miss any of your favorite bands. Talk about efficient time management!

If you are driving to the festival, or your folks are driving you, you may want to consider carpooling with other friends or family members. It's an easy way to be nice to the environment. Also, be sure to hang a "Carpoolchella" sign in your vehicle if you have four or more people with you. (If one of the Coachella carpool spotters sees you, you may get hooked up with Coachella passes for life!)

Be sure that you have enough money with you for food and water and to shop at some of the incredible vendor booths located throughout the festival grounds. Good news for your wallet: Coachella prides itself on keeping its vendor prices low so you can get more bang for your buck. It's important to remember that Coachella is a cash-only festival. Food, drink, and merchandise vendors can accept only cash, so leave the credit card at home. However, you can find an ATM machine on site. Check the weather before you go. If you go to www.coachella.com, you can find the local weather forecast for Coachella Valley. There is a good chance that it's going to be hot in the day and cool at night, so don't forget the sunscreen and a hat. Stash some warmer clothes in your backpack for when it cools down at night. In the rare event that it looks like rain, bring an extra T-shirt and shorts as well. Wear comfortable shoes and pack lightly because you will be doing a lot of walking around.

You never know if the only available spot to see your favorite band will be right in front of massive speakers, so pack a pair of earplugs just in case the show gets too loud. Don't forget to charge your cell phone and bring it with you. If you don't have a phone, consider borrowing one. There aren't any pay phones on the festival site, so be sure someone with you has a cell phone. If you're not driving, make sure you have a ride home from the festival and confirm that they know exactly when and where to pick you up.

Finally, don't forget your tickets. You don't want to drive all the way to the show, only to discover that you left them at home. If you are picking up your tickets at the venue, make sure that you call before the show and find out where you need to go to get them. Don't forget identification. You will need it in order to pick up your tickets.

Rules and Regulations

The Coachella Festival is not just another music festival—for many people it has become the reason for an annual trek to the desert.

The Coachella Festival is one of the best organized music festivals in the world. The promoters and their staff work very hard each year to make sure that everyone who attends the festival has a safe, fun, and memorable experience. The following is a list of all rules and regulations that apply at the festival. You can also find a set of these rules online at www.coachella.com, and they are posted on the festival grounds as well:

- NO instruments
- NO knives, weapons, etc.
- NO chains, chain wallets
- NO blankets
- NO outside food and beverages
- NO camelbacks (backpack canteens)
- NO tents (inside the festival grounds)
- NO flags
- NO refunds or exchanges
- NO chairs
- NO video cameras
- NO audio recording devices
- NO bota bags (leather canteens)

A refreshing squirt of cool water is always welcomed by Coachella fans. Festival organizers do all they can to keep attendees happy, safe, and comfortable.

- NO professional cameras
- NO stuffed animals
- NO pets
- ABSOLUTELY NO drugs and/or drug paraphernalia

- OK backpacks (medium)
- OK hats
- OK sunglasses
- OK sunblock/lip balm
- OK cell phone
- OK small beach towel
- OK fanny packs
- OK digital/disposable cameras

Coachella is an all-ages show, with children five years old and younger admitted free of charge. The gates open at 11:00 AM each day, and the festival runs through midnight. If you need to pick up your tickets, the box office opens at 9:00 AM. Parking is always free at Coachella, and the festival takes place rain or shine. Keep in mind that there are no "in and out" privileges, so make sure that you have everything you need for the festival before you enter. Band lineup and set times are subject to change, so check the daily schedule posted at the festival.

Knowing the rules and regulations of the Coachella Festival before you go will make you better prepared and more aware of what to expect. Have fun!

CHAPTER 5

THE FUTURE LOOKS BRIGHT FOR COACHELLA

Since its beginning in 1999, when the first festival attracted approximately twenty-five thousand people, the Coachella Valley Music and Arts Festival has evolved into one of the most popular and respected music and arts festivals in the world.

Reunion Rumors:
Bands That May Reunite to Play Coachella

Coachella has a successful track record of bringing favorite bands from the 1980s and 1990s out of retirement to perform at the festival. Reunion performances at Coachella have frequently resulted in exciting reunion tours and recordings. Bands such as Jane's Addiction, the Pixies, Iggy and the Stooges, New Order, Crowded House, Daft Punk, the Jesus and Mary Chain, and Rage Against the Machine have dusted off their instruments

Zack de la Rocha *(left)* and Tom Morello of Rage Against the Machine are shown here. This reunion appearance at Coachella 2007 was highly anticipated.

and thrilled the crowds of Coachella.

Which bands might be coaxed out of retirement to play the festival in the years to come? Unfortunately, it looks as though Coachella will not be the site of a reunion of the Smiths, one of the most important alternative rock bands to emerge from the British music scene in the 1980s. The publicist for the Smiths' lead singer, Morrissey (who has gone on to enjoy a highly successful solo career), confirmed that the singer turned down a multimillion-dollar offer to reform the Smiths and play at the 2008 Coachella Festival.

However, the British alternative band Portishead was confirmed as the 2008 festival headliners, following a decade of inactivity, and many other bands may potentially reunite at upcoming festivals. Among the most hyped names appearing on Coachella message boards, in music magazines, and in fan chat rooms are My Bloody Valentine, Pavement, the Specials, Blur, and the Afghan Whigs.

How Can I Attend the Coachella Festival?

Now that you have learned about the Coachella Festival, you may want to check it out. If you don't live near Indio, California, you will need to make travel plans. Figure out whether you can get to the festival by car, or if you will need to travel by train, bus, or plane. Also, if you are staying for the entire festival (it's three days long), you will need someplace to stay overnight. If you're under the age of eighteen, you can't camp on the Coachella Festival grounds. However, there are lots of hotels and offsite campgrounds near the festival grounds. Check the phone book in Indio, the Internet, or www.coachella.com for some recommendations. Remember that Coachella is likely to sell out every year, so the earlier that you can start planning to attend, the better. Check with your parents or another responsible adult to help you plan your trip, and set a budget. It may take some work to get to Coachella, but it's definitely worth it.

When it comes to scoring tickets, your first stop should be www.coachella.com. This is the best place to go once you have decided you want to attend. It's updated all year long and will keep you in the know regarding the bands that are slated to play, as well as the special contests and events that are running

Nothing is impossible at Coachella! Wayne Coyne, lead singer of the Flaming Lips, crowd-surfs in a giant plastic bubble at the 2004 Coachella Festival.

and other fun stuff. Most important, this is where you can pre-order tickets to the festival. Once the festival lineup is set, it is posted on the Web site, along with instructions on how to pre-order tickets. Note that if you are planning to pre-order, you will need to pay by credit card, so get the OK from a parent or guardian before you do this. Generally, most people buy the three-day pass package, which gets you admission to the entire festival, including access to all of the music. The three-day pass is expensive (close to three hundred dollars in 2007), but it is less expensive than buying three single-day passes.

If you are not able to pre-order your tickets, you may still be able to get tickets up to the day of the show at Ticketmaster outlets. Check online (www.ticketmaster.com) to find a

Ticketmaster location near you. Remember that in addition to the regular price of the ticket, Ticketmaster will add a service charge.

You may be able to purchase tickets the day of the show at the venue box office. The three-day pass packages almost always sell out before the show, so you will probably just get to go to one day of the festival if you wait this long. Check the Web site, and call the information line before you drive all the way to Indio, only to find out that it's entirely sold out.

Also, you can check online or in the city where you live for ticket brokers and ticket agencies. Generally, ticket brokers have tickets for concerts, festivals, and sporting events all over the country, even if the event is sold out. However, going through ticket brokers is usually expensive, so always verify their prices before you purchase tickets from them, either in person or online.

Remember, the Coachella Festival is one of the most anticipated music festivals of the year, which people from around the world want to come and enjoy. If you decide that you want to go, your best bet is to buy your tickets early. Start checking the Web site three or four months prior to the festival. When the tickets go on sale, empty your piggy bank and get them before they are gone!

GLOSSARY

ample More than enough; fully sufficient to meet a need or purpose.

contemporary Current, modern.

cuisine Style or quality of cooking.

debacle Disaster or complete failure.

diva Distinguished female singer.

diverse Different; differing one from another.

drastically Severely or radically; extremely.

emit To give forth or release (a sound).

fiasco Complete failure.

genre Type or category.

interactive Acting upon or with.

literally Really, actually.

mirage Illusion caused by the heat of a desert.

Mojave Desert Area in Southern California and western Arizona.

regulations Principles, rules, or laws designed to control.

reunion Gathering of the members of a group who have been separated.

screening Showing of a film.

trek Journey or trip.

visionary One whose ideas are futuristic, dreamy, or impractical.

City of Indio, California Chamber of Commerce
82921 Indio Boulevard
Indio, CA 92201
(760) 342-0676
Web site: http://www.indiochamber.org
Contact the Indio Chamber of Commerce for answers to all
   questions regarding Indio's business community.

Goldenvoice
5750 Wilshire Boulevard, Suite 501
Los Angeles, CA 90036
(323) 930-5700
Web site: http://www.goldenvoice.com
Goldenvoice is the main promoter of the Coachella Valley
   Music and Arts Festival.

Rolling Stone
1290 Avenue of the Americas
New York, NY 10104-0298
(212) 484-1616
Web site: http://www.rollingstone.com
Rolling Stone magazine covers all types of music and related
   concerts and events.

Web Sites

Due to the changing nature of Internet links, Rosen Publishing has developed an online list of Web sites related to the subject of this book. This site is updated regularly. Please use this link to access the list:

http://www.rosenlinks.com/mmf/coac

FOR FURTHER READING

Anderson, Stephen. *So, You Wanna Be a Rock Star?: How to Create Music, Get Gigs, and Maybe Even Make It Big!* Hillsboro, OR: Beyond Words Publishing, Inc., 1999.

Pyle, Linda McMillin, and Evelyn Tschida McMillin. *Peaks, Palms & Picnics: Day Journeys in the Mountains and Deserts of Palm Springs and the Coachella Valley of Southern California.* El Cajon, CA: Sunbelt Publications, 2002.

Reisfeld, Randi. *This Is the Sound: The Best of Alternative Music.* New York, NY: Simon Pulse, 1996.

Taylor, Steve. *The A to X of Alternative Music.* New York, NY: Continuum International Publishing Group, 2006.

BIBLIOGRAPHY

Brooklyn Vegan. "Coachella: April 25–27, 2008 . . . Who Will Reunite?" Retrieved November 30, 2007 (http://www.brooklynvegan.com/archives/2007/11/coachella_april.html).

Caldwell, June. "Coachella Music Festival 2006 Review." *American Chronicle*, May 7, 2006. Retrieved November 29, 2007 (http://www.americanchronicle.com/articles/viewarticle.asp?articleid=9144).

Cohen, Jonathan. "Morrissey Rewards Diehards, Quashes Smiths Reunion." Billboard.com, August 23, 2007. Retrieved December 4, 2007 (http://www.billboard.com/bbcom/news/article_display.jsp?vhv_contentid=100363017).

Collins, Robert. "Been Caught Healing: An Interview with Perry Farrell." *PopMatters*, July 6, 2007. Retrieved November 30, 2007 (http://www.popmatters.com/pm/features/articles/43535/been-caught-healing-an-interview-with-perry-farrell).

TDS editors. "Believe It or Not: My Bloody Valentine Reuniting for Coachella 2008?" *The Daily Swarm*, August 26, 2007. Retrieved December 4, 2007 (http://www.thedailyswarm.com/swarm/believe_it_or_not_my_bloody_valentine_reuniting_for_coachela_2008).

U.S. Music Vault. "Woodstock 1999: What Happened?" Retrieved November 29, 2007 (http://www.usmusicvault.com/woodstock99.html).

COACHELLA

T

Tool, 6, 7, 9, 10, 18, 21

W

Woodstock 1999, 8–9

About the Author

Greg Robison has been actively involved in the music industry for the past fifteen years. He is the cofounder of an independent record label, has served as a band manager and consultant, and has promoted numerous concerts and special music events. In addition to this title, he is also the author of *Vans Warped Tour*, *Ozzfest*, and *Christian Rock Festivals*, all published by Rosen. He and his wife, Kelly, live in Texas.

Photo Credits

Cover (all photos), pp. 1 (all photos except bottom right), 4 (left and right), 10, 12, 14, 19, 22, 25, 32, 38, 40 © Getty Images; p. 1 (bottom right), back cover © www.istockphoto.com/Milan Klusacek; p. 8 © Neal Preston/Corbis; p. 17 Sam Zavieh; pp. 28, 35 © AP Photo.

Designer: Nelson Sá; Editor: Christopher Roberts
Photo Researcher: Marty Levick